ARE YOU
READY?

I SPY with my little eye, something beginning with...

A is for Alien

I SPY with my little eye, something beginning with...

B is for Black hole

I SPY with my little eye, something beginning with...

C is for Comet

I SPY with my little eye,
something beginning with...
D

D is for

Dark Energy star

I SPY with my little eye, something beginning with...
E

E is for
Earth

I SPY with my little eye, something beginning with...

F is for Flag in moon

I SPY with my little eye, something beginning with...

G is for Galaxy Spiral

I SPY with my little eye,
something beginning with...
OH

H is for Half Moon

I SPY with my little eye,
something beginning with...
I

I is for Irregular Galaxy

I SPY with my little eye, something beginning with...

J is for Jupiter

I SPY with my little eye, something beginning with...

K is for K-Type Star

I SPY with my little eye, something beginning with...

is for
Landing Capsule

I SPY with my little eye,
something beginning with...

M is for Moon

I SPY with my little eye,
something beginning with...
ON

N is for Neptune

I SPY with my little eye, something beginning with...

is for
Observatory

I SPY with my little eye,
something beginning with...

P is for Planet and moon

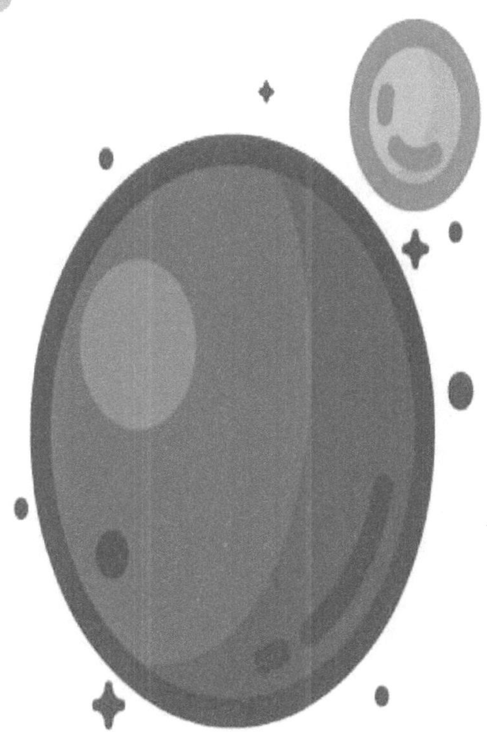

I SPY with my little eye,
something beginning with...
R

R is for Rocket

I SPY with my little eye, something beginning with...

S is for Satelite

I SPY with my little eye, something beginning with...

T is for
Telescope

I SPY with my little eye,
something beginning with...

U is for
Urenus

I SPY with my little eye, something beginning with...
W

W is for
Wolf-Rayet Star

I SPY with my little eye, something beginning with...

Y is for Yellow Alien

I SPY with my little eye,
something beginning with...
ZO

Z is for Zytkow Object

Thank You for buying this book. I hope you liked the product. If you can, leave your feedback because it helps me develop a lot. You can also see my other products - Have Fun!